HORSES
and Ponies

Peter Gray

W
FRANKLIN WATTS
LONDON • SYDNEY

First published in 2013 by Franklin Watts

Copyright © 2013 Arcturus Publishing Limited

Franklin Watts
338 Euston Road
London NW1 3BH

Franklin Watts Australia
Level 17/207 Kent Street, Sydney NSW 2000

Produced by Arcturus Publishing Limited,
26/27 Bickels Yard, 151–153 Bermondsey Street, London SE1 3HA

Illustrations: © Peter Gray
Editors: Joe Harris and Nicola Barber
Design: sprout.uk.com
Cover design: sprout.uk.com

A CIP catalogue record for this book is available from the British Library.

Dewey Decimal Classification Number 743.6'96655

ISBN 978 1 4451 1876 5

Printed in China

Franklin Watts is a division of Hachette Children's Books, an Hachette UK company.
www.hachette.co.uk

SL002689EN

Supplier 03, Date 0513, Print Run 2385

CONTENTS

DRAWING

You should start your drawings with simple guidelines before fleshing them out with detail.

Build up the general shape of your subject with guidelines. I have drawn the guidelines quite heavily to make them easy to follow, but you should work faintly with a hard pencil.

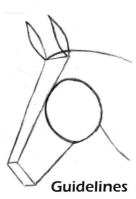

Guidelines

Use a softer pencil to develop the character and details. You may find that you do not follow the

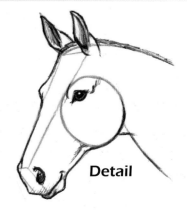

Detail

guidelines exactly in places. That's fine – they are only a rough guide.

Carefully erase the guidelines and mistakes. Then add shading and **texture** with a soft pencil.

Shading and texture

INKING

For a bold look, go over the outlines with ink. Wait for the ink to dry thoroughly, then erase all the pencil marks.

Felt-tip pen outlines

The easiest inking method is to use a felt-tip pen. If you plan to add paint at a later stage, make sure your pen is waterproof.

For a more graceful effect, use a fine-tipped watercolour brush dipped in ink.

Brush outlines

COLOURING

Although I use watercolours in this book, the main principles are the same for any materials – start with the shading, then add in markings and textures, and finally work your main colours over the top.

Felt-tip colouring

Felt-tip pens produce bright, vibrant colours. Work quickly to avoid the pen strokes remaining visible.

Coloured pencils

Coloured pencils are the easiest colouring tools to use, but you have to take great care to blend the colours to achieve a good finish.

Watercolours

The subtlest effects can be achieved with watercolour paints. It is best to buy them as a set of solid blocks that you wet with a brush. Mix the colours in a palette or on an old white plate.

HEAD SHAPE

The horse has a long and narrow head. Here are some tips for getting its shape right.

These are the basic guidelines for a horse's head. The nose is long and straight, and the neck is broad. Draw a circle for the cheek. This circle will help you to position the eye correctly.

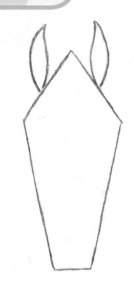

A front view shows you the width of the animal's head between its eyes. The lower part of the head is much narrower.

A good way to get the nostrils right is to think of the left one as a number '6' and the right one as its mirror image. Note how close together the ears sit at the top of the head.

As you work on the outlines, you will see how closely they follow the guidelines. The nose is rounded out and the chin extends down a little. The eye, ear and mane will need some more detail.

Dished face   **Roman nose**

VARIATIONS
The basic face shape varies in different breeds of horses and ponies. Noses may be longer or shorter. Heads may be thinner or broader.

These are two quite extreme versions, one with a 'dished' face (an upturned nose), and the other with a downturned or 'Roman' nose.

BODY SHAPE

Here we look at the horse's body structure in three different ways.

This diagram shows the way that a horse's body can be measured in head lengths. An average horse is about three head lengths tall at the shoulder. Its torso (main body) is also three head lengths long. However, these **proportions** can be different for horses of different breeds and ages.

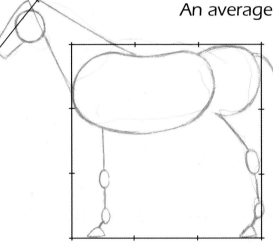

Proportions

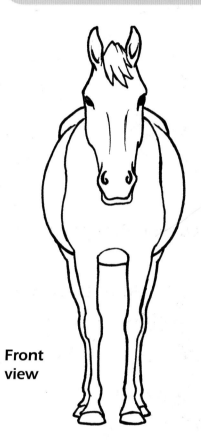

Front view

This skeleton view of a horse should help you to make sense of the joints. The shoulderbones push forwards from the chest and the hips angle backwards. Notice where the joints are found in the legs.

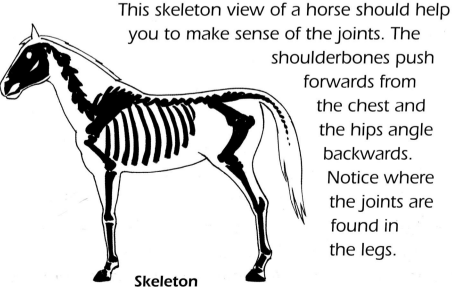

Skeleton

Viewed from the front, you can see that the shoulders are narrow, the hips wider and the belly rounded and broad. Note how close together the legs are on the ground.

A thoroughbred is a breed of horse used for racing, jumping and other **equestrian** sports. Thoroughbreds are usually agile, quick and lively.

1 Begin by drawing a large oval with a flat top. This is the main part of the horse's chest and belly. Add a small circle for the head, and a long curve off the animal's rear end for its **rump**. Leave enough space on the paper for the legs and tail.

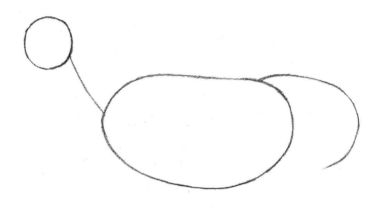

2 Draw the cone shape of the **muzzle** and then add a line for the back of the neck, arching over the head. Sketch in the long, thin curves of the legs, which become narrower towards the feet.

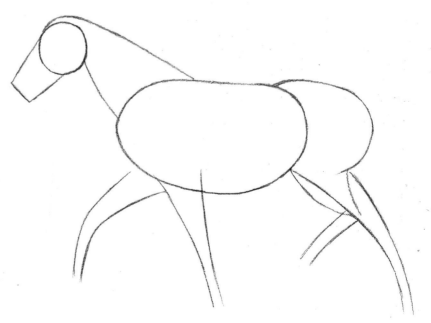

3 Horses' legs have visible joints, which look quite knobbly. It's a good idea to draw fairly large ovals on the legs for each joint, taking care to place them correctly. Sketch out the mane and tail as simple shapes without texture or detail.

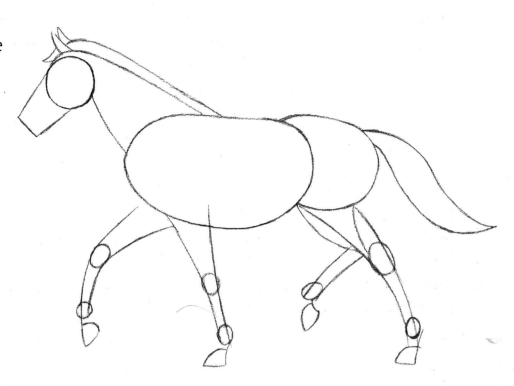

4 Now that the guidelines are finished, you can start on the details. Draw the main features of the face and the shape of the harness. Work on the upper legs. Note the bulky shoulder area at the front of the chest above the leading (front) leg.

5 Work on the detail using a sharp pencil and an eraser. Make the body curves smooth and graceful, and pay attention to the muscles and joints of the legs. Work on the head and harness and add some flowing texture to the mane and tail.

6 Once you are happy with your outlines, it's time to ink them in. Use fine, confident strokes. Move the paper around on your desk to allow your arm to work freely. When the ink is dry, all the pencil work can be erased to leave a clean outline.

7 You can break the colouring process down into stages. For this horse, I decided to start with the dark markings. I mixed dark brown and blue to make black. Where the markings blend into the upper leg, I used a dampened brush to soften the hard edge of the paint marks. I also added some shading to the ankles and hooves.

FAMOUS HORSES

Thoroughbreds are ridden by people in a wide range of sporting events. Many of them are trained to be racers – either on flat courses with no jumps, or in races with fences and ditches. The most successful of these horses have become racing legends, with names such as Seabiscuit, Red Rum and Desert Orchid.

ANIMAL FACTS

8 To add shading to the body, I mixed up a warm dark brown colour. I used this colour for the darkest areas, under the belly and inside the legs. Where the shading was less dark, I watered down the paint. Then I softened the edges of the painted areas with a wet brush and clean tissue paper.

9 Once the shading is complete, wash the main colour on in broad strokes. Keep the paint flowing and do not allow any hard edges to become dry as you work. When the area is covered, allow it to dry completely.

10 Once the paint is dry, you can add other small areas of colour and strengthen the shading. Then work on the sheen to make the horse look glossy. I wet the areas of **highlight** with a brush, then dabbed off the moistened paint with a clean tissue. You might prefer to create highlights with watered-down white ink or chalk. Add a few spots of white ink to bring out the highlights on the head.

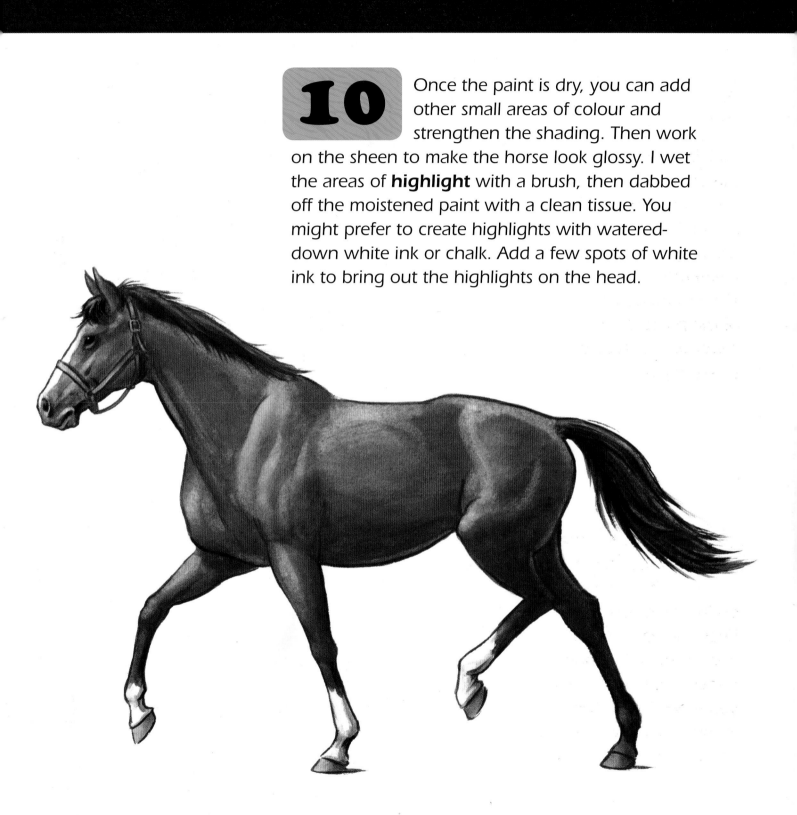

FOAL

A foal is a baby horse, up to one year old. Foals have very long legs and small, slim bodies. Their manes and tails are short. After its first birthday, a foal is known as a yearling.

1 Although a foal is much leaner than a fully-grown horse, you start with a similar oval for the chest and belly. Add a circle for the head and a long curve off the animal's rear end for its rump.

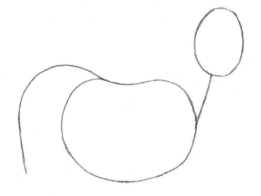

2 Draw in the muzzle and the neck, arching over the head. Sketch in the legs, which are very long and thin in a foal.

LONG LEGS

When a foal is born, its legs are almost as long as they will be when it has grown into an adult horse. Unlike human babies, foals use their legs almost straight away. A foal will be standing within an hour of birth, and by one day old it will be trotting and galloping next to its mother.

3 Draw the head as a roughly rectangular box at this stage. The knees are very knobbly and the tail and mane are short. To place the legs firmly on the ground, draw a neat shape on the floor to guide you.

4 Now draw in the main features of the face and the ears. Work on the upper legs, bringing out the curves of the foal's muscles. Add some detail to the hooves.

5 Continue working on the detail of the head, mane and short tail. Make the body curves smooth and pay attention to the joints on the foal's long legs.

6 To give a softer feel for this young animal, I decided on coloured ink for part of the outline. I used a yellow-brown colour for the body and upper legs, and black ink for the darker parts.

7 Although the nose is as dark as the legs and tail, it is more grey in colour. A young horse is not as sleek and shiny as an adult. To give a sense of the fluffier coat, I painted some short, soft strokes on the foal's body.

WILD HORSE

Most of the wild horses around the world are related to **domesticated** animals that escaped or strayed. These horses have gone back to the wild, where they usually live in small groups.

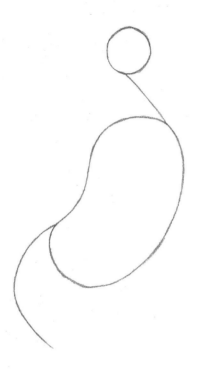

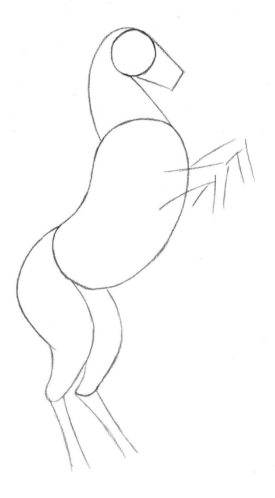

1 This wild horse is up on its hind legs, so position the large oval of the body at an angle. The head circle sits on top, and the line of the animal's rear end curves in below.

2 Draw the cone shape of the muzzle and then add the line for the back of the neck, arching over the head. Add the angles of the two front legs. The powerful back legs reach down to the ground.

WHITE HORSES

Camargue horses get their name from an area of southern France, where they live in the marshes and wetlands. These small horses date back to ancient times. They all have completely white coats with black skin beneath. This colour of horse is known as a 'grey'.

ANIMAL FACTS

3 Draw large ovals on the legs for each joint, and hooves on the ends of the legs. Add the general shapes of the ears, mane and tail.

4 Now start work on the details of the face and the rearing front legs. Add some basic texture to the mane and tail.

5 Work on the outlines and details using a sharp pencil. Make the body curves smooth and the rear legs strong and powerful.

6 For the inking stage I used black ink. But for a softer feel to the upper surfaces and hair, I dipped the black-loaded brush in water to dilute the ink.

7 This is a white horse (a 'grey'), but you still need to use some colour. For most of the shading I used blue paint mixed with a small amount of brown to make grey. For the horse's underside I used a yellow-brown to suggest colour reflected from a sandy ground surface. There is also a hint of yellow in the creamier colour of the mane and tail, and some yellow in the brown of the hooves.

WILD PONY

Wild ponies are usually quite broad and sturdy animals, with short legs. Their coats are fairly coarse and thick to keep them warm in winter, and they have long manes and tails. These hardy little ponies have to be able to survive all weathers.

1 This wild pony is a much sturdier creature than the others in this book, so make the oval of the body extra deep and rounded. Add a circle for the head.

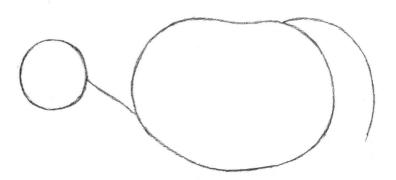

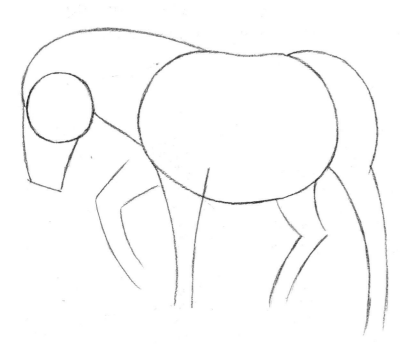

2 Draw the cone shape of the muzzle, and a line to indicate the neck. The neck is wide and strong. The legs are short and thick.

3 Add the details of the ears, mane and tail. Sketch in the big, sturdy leg joints. They are quite close to each other because of the pony's short legs.

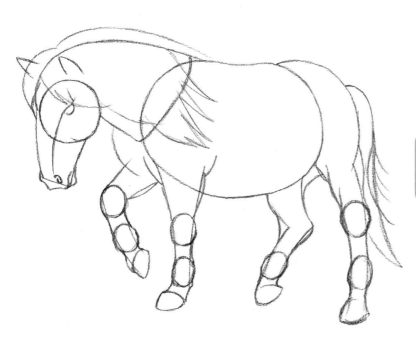

4 Draw the main features of the face and sketch in some detail for the mane and tail. Work on the upper parts of the legs, bringing out the curves of the muscles.

SHIPWRECKED PONIES

Chincoteague ponies live on a long island just off the eastern coast of the United States. According to legend, these wild ponies found their way to the island when Spanish ships were wrecked off the coast in the 1500s! But it's more likely that they were brought to the island by farmers, then left to run wild.

ANIMAL FACTS

5 I wanted to make the hair look windswept, so I drew the general flow of its movement. Don't try to put in every detail – it will look more natural to ink and paint the hair in the next stages. I also added a suggestion of scruffy hair around the hooves and lower legs.

6 I inked the flyaway hair in swift strokes with black ink diluted with water. A small amount of ink on the brush allows the texture of the brush hairs to show. I made the general outlines quite rough to capture the shaggy appearance of the pony's coat.

7 Once I had coloured and shaded the animal, I added lots of fine strokes to capture the texture of the coat. This pony's rough coat has little natural sheen, so I kept the highlights to a minimum on the body. I used white ink for the mane and tail and the shaggy legs.

Now it's time to test your skills by putting some of the horses in this book into a suitable scene. You can choose any of the different kinds of horses we have drawn.

1 When you are creating a scene, it is a good idea to start with a rough version of your artwork. I decided to set two wild ponies against a background scene of windswept moors. I created a rough drawing and worked out a shading scheme, with the light coming from the right-hand side, and a dark, stormy sky.

2 To work out a rough colour scheme, quickly apply some colour to your pencil rough. I chose to use the colours of autumn – yellows, greens and browns, with a heavy purple-grey sky.

3 Once the paint is dry, develop your colour rough with some dark outlining. I decided to make the distant pony dark in colour to stand out against its pale background. I also darkened the sky and some of the shadows, and added a few bright highlights with white ink.

4 On a large sheet of good paper, draw the guidelines for your final picture. Apart from the ponies, there was little detailed drawing required for my scene, but I sketched in the general forms of the landscape.

5 Work some more pencil detail into the scene, including all the marks you will need for inking. I completed the drawings of the ponies and worked on the general textures of the landscape. Rather than draw every stone in the wall, I made marks to guide my inking brush.

6 Now it's time for inking. I inked in the trees over the rough pencil marks, as well as the wall and the grass, all rather loosely. I took more care over the ponies. Then I marked in the distant horizon with a few swift strokes of thinly diluted ink.

7 Before starting on the colour, I worked on the dark areas of the picture. I mixed two shades of dark grey out of blue, dark red and brown. Then I painted them over the sky area with a large brush. I used the same colour for the darker areas of shading on the animals.

8 For the colour, I mixed up several grass colours using greens, browns and yellows. I painted them quickly over the grass, for a feel of rough, scrubby grassland. I darkened the sky and the horse's shadows a little more. Then I worked up the **foreground**, using more inks, both black and white, to strengthen and develop the various textures.

GLOSSARY

domesticated Describes an animal that has been tamed and adapted by humans to work for them.

equestrian Relating to or involving horses.

foreground The front part of a picture.

highlight A bright area in a painting or drawing.

muzzle The nose and mouth of an animal such as a horse, cat or dog.

proportion The size of one thing in relation to another.

rump The back part of the body of an animal.

texture The feel of a surface.

WEBSITES

http://www.discoverhorses.com/
A site about horses and riding. The children's section features book reviews and quizzes.

http://www.horse-games.org
Horse-themed facts, games and stories.

FURTHER READING

All About Drawing Horses and Pets by Russell Farrell (Walter Foster, 2009)

The Allen Book of Painting and Drawing Horses by Jennifer Bell (J A Allen & Co Ltd, 2011)

How to Draw Horses (Young Artist) by Lucy Smith (Usbourne, 2006)

The Kingfisher Illustrated Horse and Pony Encyclopedia by Sandy Ransford (Kingfisher, 2010)

INDEX